Key Stage 2 English Creative Writing

WORKBOOK **1**

Short Story Writing

Dr Stephen C Curran

Edited by Andrea Richardson and Warren Vokes

This book belongs to

Accelerated Education Publications Ltd

Contents

1. Story Starting Points   **Pages**

1. The Five Senses   3-4
2. Images, Sounds, Objects, Smells and Tastes   4-5
3. The Sixth Sense (Feelings)   5-6
4. Brainstorming Ideas   6-8
5. 'Stream of Consciousness'   9-10
6. Writing in Role   10-11
7. Special Memories   12-13
8. Characters from People you know   14-16
9. Dramatic Life Events   16-19
10. Literature and Other Sources   19-21

1st Draft of Story 1 - *The Room*   22-31
1st Draft of Story 2 - *Trapped*

2. Literary Devices

1. Developing Description   32-34
2. The Flashback   34-36
3. The Flashforward   36-38
4. Tension   39-40
5. Suspense   40-42
6. Anticipation   42-44
7. Mood   44-46
8. Atmosphere   46-48
9. Conflict   49-50
10. Surprise   51-52
11. Intrigue or Curiosity   53-56

2nd Draft of Story 1 - *The Room*   57-66
2nd Draft of Story 2 - *Trapped*

© 2008 Stephen Curran

Chapter One
Story Starting Points
1. The Five Senses

Human beings receive information from the world around them through the **Five Senses**. These senses could be called the 'gateways to the soul' because they are the means by which we connect with the inner person. They are as follows:

Sight • **Hearing** • **Touch** • **Smell** • **Taste**

Exercise 1: 1   Try this experiment to engage two of your senses right now.

1) Look around you; where you are right now and see if you notice one thing you have not seen before. _____

2) Close your eyes right now and listen for one sound you have not heard before in the space you are in. _____

Every day our senses receive huge amounts of information. Successful writing involves being able to use and organise this information creatively. It is important to think about our experiences and the information we receive through each sense.

Exercise 1: 2   Describe three distinct things you have experienced today through each sense.

Today I have seen: e.g. a car 1. _____

_____ 2. _____

_____ 3. _____

Today I have heard: e.g. an aeroplane 1. _____

_____ 2. _____

_____ 3. _____

© 2008 Stephen Curran

Today I have touched: e.g. a pencil 1. _____

_____ 2. _____

_____ 3. _____

Today I have smelt: e.g. perfume 1. _____

_____ 2. _____

_____ 3. _____

Today I have tasted: e.g. cereal 1. _____

_____ 2. _____

_____ 3. _____

2. Images, Sounds, Objects, Smells and Tastes

Our life experiences provide us with pleasurable (positive) and painful (negative) memories which are useful for writing purposes. These life experiences are perceived through our five senses and give rise to feelings and reactions.

Examples: | Experiences perceived through the five senses.

Perceived by Sight - An image - *'A beautiful sunset.'*
Hearing - A sound - *'The singing of a nightingale.'*
Touch - An object - *'The soft fur of the family cat.'*
Smell - An aroma - *'The strong smell of cleaning fluid.'*
Taste - A flavour - *'The delicate taste of milk chocolate.'*

Exercise 1: 3

Descriptively list five of your own experiences of each of the following.

Five Images: 1. _____

© 2008 Stephen Curran

2. _____ 3. _____

4. _____ 5. _____

Five Sounds: 1. _____

2. _____ 3. _____

4. _____ 5. _____

Five Objects: 1. _____

2. _____ 3. _____

4. _____ 5. _____

Five Aromas: 1. _____

2. _____ 3. _____

4. _____ 5. _____

Five Flavours: 1. _____

2. _____ 3. _____

4. _____ 5. _____

3. The Sixth Sense (Feelings)

Everybody has **Feelings** but they cannot be seen. They can only be shown by the way people behave.

If the characters in stories experience feelings, the readers of those stories can experience them too.

Information absorbed by the five senses gives rise to various feelings within people. These feelings are often called intuition or the **Sixth Sense**.

Example: | What feelings do we all experience? |

Our feelings can include: *anger; delight; depression; fear; thoughtfulness; reflection; excitement; distress; melancholy.*
Extreme feelings can include: *rage; terror; despair; bliss; joy.*

© 2008 Stephen Curran

Exercise 1: 4

List nine more feelings we all experience during our lives.

1. _____ 2. _____ 3. _____

4. _____ 5. _____ 6. _____

7. _____ 8. _____ 9. _____

It is important to make characters in stories continually react to each other. These feelings can only be expressed when the characters take action in relation to other characters.

Example: In what ways do characters show their feelings?

Characters in stories might demonstrate their feelings by: *smiling; laughing; grinning; hiding; blushing; stamping their feet; jumping up and down; slamming doors; running away; turning away; looking down; throwing things;* etc.

Exercise 1: 5

Think of ten more things a character might do to show their feelings.

1. _____   6. _____

2. _____   7. _____

3. _____   8. _____

4. _____   9. _____

5. _____   10. _____

4. Brainstorming Ideas

One approach is to **Brainstorm**, or list any ideas, once a story title or particular character is decided upon.

© 2008 Stephen Curran

Example:  Write any words, phrases or sentences that come come into mind with the story title ***Time Ran Out***.

We might use the following words, phrases or sentences:
Words - 'speed'; 'rushing'; 'danger'; 'fear'; 'desperate'
Phrases - 'engine spluttered'; 'wrong key'; 'inner panic'
Sentences - 'His arm bled profusely.' 'The car turned over.'

Exercise 1: 6
Write any words, phrases or sentences that come into your mind with one of the following titles.

Try ***The Beast***, ***The Message***, ***The Narrow Escape***, ***My Worst Fear***, ***The Nightmare*** or ***The Joke***.
Or you could try characters such as: a **tramp**, a **king**, an **actor**, a **doctor**, a **detective**, a **pilot** or a **train driver**.

Seven Words: 1. _____ 2. _____ 3. _____

4. _____ 5. _____ 6. _____ 7. _____

Five Phrases: 1. _____ 2. _____

3. _____ 4. _____ 5. _____

_____

Three Sentences: 1. _____

2. _____

3. _____

Spider Diagrams or **Brain Maps** can help you brainstorm your thoughts and ideas and organise them on paper.

Example:  Create a spider diagram or brain map for the story title ***The Mighty Storm at Sea***.

We could use the six senses and write words and phrases.

© 2008 Stephen Curran

Spider diagrams or mind maps can be used to stimulate story ideas. They can have various categories. For example, the **Five Elements of Story** are:

Where • When • Who • What • Why

Another possibility is to use story subject areas:

Theme • Storyline • Event • Character • Issue • Memory

Exercise 1: 7

Add some more words or phrases to this spider diagram for the story title *The Dark Caves*.

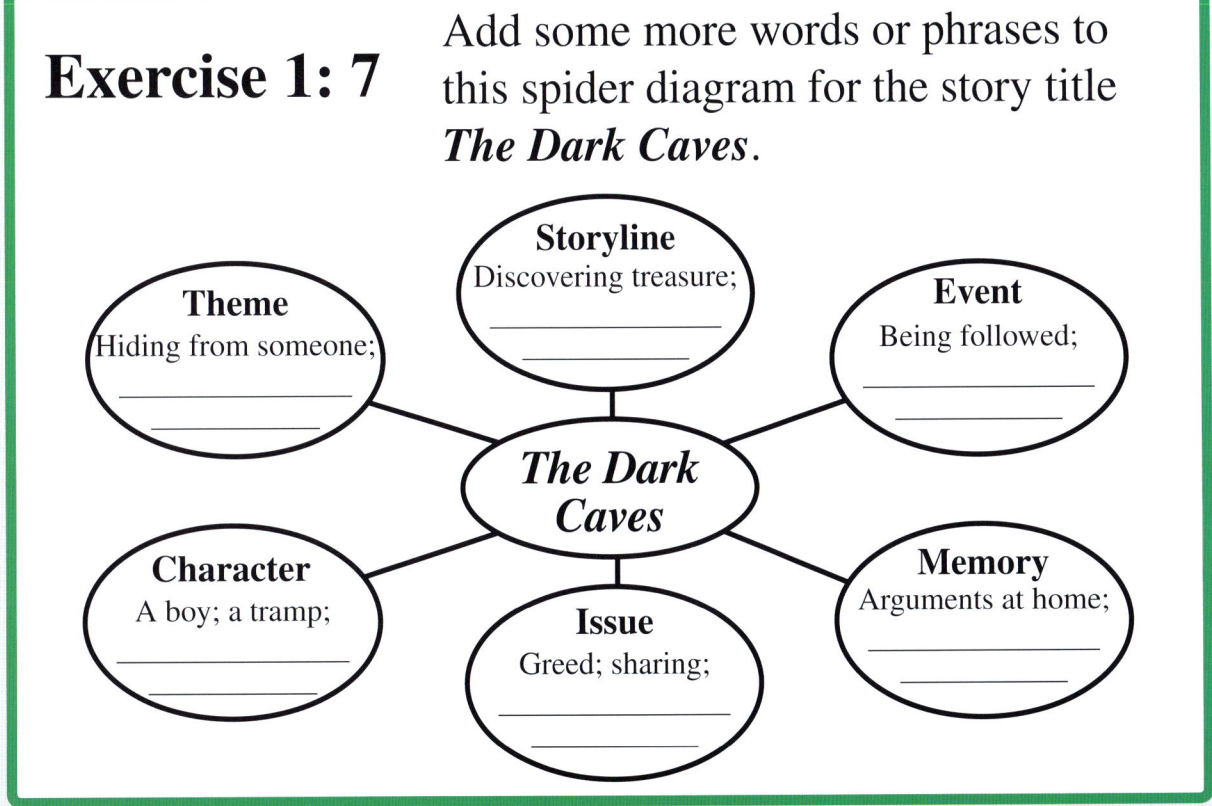

5. 'Stream of Consciousness'

This involves writing any ideas or thoughts that come into the mind at speed without editing them. Many useless things may be written, but amongst these words there may be ideas that can be used. A **'Stream of Consciousness'** can begin with a word, phrase or sentence.

Example: Write a 'stream of consciousness' for a story entitled *Secret Places*.

This is a 'stream of consciousness' for *Secret Places*. No editing has taken place.

'I went to my secret place today. It was cold and windy as I stood on the edge of the cliff. I looked longingly out towards the horizon, because I always wanted to go to sea and work on a ship. What a wonderful life to be free; to watch the sunset every night and see the sunrise every morning. If they won't train me as a sailor, I could work as a waiter or even clean the cabins. Maybe I could work as an entertainer as I can sing, dance and act. I cannot let my dream slip away.'

Exercise 1: 8   Choose one of these titles and write a 'stream of consciousness': *The Pet from Hell*, *Lost* or *The Tunnel*.

_____

_____

_____

_____

_____

© 2008 Stephen Curran

_____

_____

_____

_____

_____

6. Writing in Role

This is a development of the 'stream of consciousness' idea. A particular character is imagined and their thoughts and feelings are written down.

If it is written in the present tense it has more immediacy and feels as if it is happening right at that moment.

Again, it is important not to edit thoughts, but just to write. Whatever material is written can be edited later.

Example:  Imagine you are a boy who is in hospital facing *The Operation* any time that day.

Writing in Role might go something like this. Remember it is written in present tense, e.g. *'I feel'* rather than *'I felt'*.

'As I lie in this hospital bed, I feel a sharp pain in my abdomen. I call it my tummy, but that's the word the doctor used. The pain's getting worse and I feel really scared. My mum's gone to buy some coffee and she says she's not worried because it's not a serious illness. How would she know? I feel like crying but I don't want them to think I'm a baby. Dad says men don't cry. I'm only a boy, but maybe he's right. The nurse with the shiny blonde hair says it won't hurt anymore if they take out my appendix, but I'm not so sure. Ouch! It really hurts.

I yell, "Nurse! Nurse!"'

10 © 2008 Stephen Curran

Exercise 1: 9

Try one of these ideas for writing in role as a character (write as if you are the person in present tense):

• a girl or boy who cannot swim, who falls into a river
• a police officer who is first on the scene of a car crash
• a fire officer rescuing a child from a burning building

7. Special Memories

This is a very useful way to start a story. Everybody has **Special Memories** of places or events. These things stay in the mind in a very vivid way. This means descriptions are likely to be full of detail and can be an inspiration to write.

Example:  Think of one special event and one special location that stands out in your memory.

Here is an example of the kind of memories of events and locations that might be fixed in a person's mind.

An event - Receiving a special award in assembly at school.
A location - A beautiful bay in North Wales.

Exercise 1: 10

Think of an event and a location that is special to you and remains very strong in your memory.

An Event: _____

A Location: _____

Example: Describe either the special event or the location in as much detail as possible.

A sunset I experienced whilst on holiday in Wales is the special event I have chosen for this description.

'I stood on a lonely deserted hill overlooking a beautiful bay in Wales. As the light began to fade I looked out to sea. The sun was a golden red as it dipped over the horizon. The lapping waters glistened as the brightness of this ancient fiery ball seemed to be quenched by the waves. Flashing orange rays splayed across a vast, cloudless and empty sky.

© 2008 Stephen Curran

I shivered a little as the source of the warmth slowly faded. The calling of the seagulls distracted me for a moment as they circled above the shimmering waters. Their white forms gracefully peppered the sky as they relentlessly scoured the surge and retreat of the tide for stranded crabs.

As the last rays of the half hidden globe traced the blue waters, every glint contained the full colours of the rainbow like a held prism turning before the light. The scene before me had been witnessed by countless generations. The day turning to night; night becoming day; for thousands of years. In those passing moments, I joined a huge crowd of witnesses and acknowledged the austere beauty and power of nature; like those before me, I stood in awe and wonder.'

Exercise 1: 11   Describe either a special location or event that is strong in your memory.

_____

_____

_____

_____

_____

_____

_____

_____

_____

_____

_____

_____

© 2008 Stephen Curran

8. Characters from People you Know

Familiar people can form the basis for characters in stories. Most authors have based their most interesting characters on people that they have come across or known very well. Sometimes a character can be composed of a combination of traits from a number of people. It is crucial never to use the real names of people that are the basis for characters. There are interesting people everywhere - **just observe**!

Example: Think of one interesting person you have known and describe them in a situation you remember.

This is a description of a teacher and an event that someone I know remembers from childhood (no real names are used).

'We could hear him coming down the corridor. There was a slow, distinct pattern to his steps. The careful lifting of each foot and swinging of his body to lift the next. We were kids and I suppose we were cruel to some extent. Mr Daniels, the music master, had a nickname; 'tin legs' on account of there being something wrong with his back and legs. We never knew what it was; perhaps an injury in some war or maybe he was born with it. It was frequently discussed.

I always thought the name was unfair; until I saw that he was cruel. He never seemed to smile except at some child's misfortune. He was merciless in his criticism if a boy could not sing in tune or answer a question correctly. Then worst of all, he could be sarcastic. You would say something and it would be twisted to mean something else and suddenly you knew he was laughing at you. There seemed to be no kindness in his eyes, although there was nothing abnormal about his face. In fact his jet black hair and

14   © 2008 Stephen Curran

chiselled chin made his features rather handsome and appealing.

I remember one incident when Daniels ordered a boy to fetch the punishment book and the cane. Timpson (we weren't called by our first names) returned without them, saying they couldn't be located. The game went on and on. Timpson was sent out, but always came back empty-handed. This was amusing until he finally returned clasping the cane and the book. Then he burst into tears and begged Daniels not to cane him. Timpson was a silly but harmless boy and we felt it was all rather unfair.

We then watched in horror as the scene played out. Timpson refusing to stand still and bend forward; then the awkward preparation as Daniels steadied himself for the huge swing.

Finally the thwack as Daniels delivered a ferocious blow, then another and another; with a cruel, sadistic grin on his face too. I had always felt some sympathy for Daniels up until that moment; but as Timpson whimpered and cried for him to stop, I could see he had no mercy. Now I loathed him!'

Exercise 1: 12

Think of an interesting character you know and a memory about them and write about it.

_____

_____

_____

_____

_____

_____

© 2008 Stephen Curran

_____

_____

_____

_____

_____

_____

_____

_____

9. Dramatic Life Events

Biographical material is sometimes interesting. However, most people's lives are made up of some interesting events and many dull and boring details which are of no interest to a reader. Alfred Hitchcock once said, 'Drama is life with the dull bits cut out'. This applies to story writing just as much. It is important to select significant events that have had some life-changing effect on a person for it to be interesting.

Example: | Write about an interesting life event that had a real impact on the way you think and behave now.

This event involved my brother and me, and through it we placed ourselves in significant danger.

'*It was the summer holiday and the days were long and hot. At first the days offered promise and freedom from the cares of school and homework; but soon my brother and I were bored and listless; that was until we came up with the idea. We would build ourselves the biggest and fastest go-cart ever. This was not a modern go-cart with an engine; the only propulsion we would need was a good slope.*

16   © 2008 Stephen Curran

My brother Peter, being ten, thought he was the best engineer going; I, at eleven, was content to direct the work and oversee the detailed plans through to implementation.

We grafted away merrily for two or three days until the 'monster' began to take shape. A six foot long heavy plank of wood, steering gear (fancy words for a bolt and crosspiece), four small bicycle wheels and a strong rope to steer the monster. It was large, heavy and impressive to look at. The only thing now was to test drive our invention.

We chose a nearby park that had a very steep hill with a winding gravel path. Peter and I climbed on without a care in the world. I took the reins and he clung on behind me. We looked forward to a fairly gentle descent, although we expected to pick up a little speed near the bottom. As we moved off everything seemed to be going to plan. The hill started gently enough and the machine was performing to expectation. It was exciting and we shouted with glee.

Then suddenly we picked up speed. It all happened so fast. Peter was screaming in my ear to stop, but I couldn't. I was terrified; it was as if our 'beast' had a life of its own. We couldn't jump; it was too dangerous and I was struggling to steer as we thundered down the hill. We knew nothing about velocity but we were about to find out what it meant. As the hill steepened we found ourselves at almost forty-five degrees, trying desperately to grip the sides of the plank. We didn't think we could go any faster, but we were wrong. I was screaming now too; we knew we would crash, but how and when we had no idea.

© 2008 Stephen Curran

As we careered towards the bottom of the slope, we saw it coming - a sudden levelling out. We spied the ditch on one side and the hard gravel path; it would be one or the other. Suddenly the front wheels twisted under the impact, the go-cart up-ended and Peter and I found ourselves flying through the air. There was a thud as we both landed awkwardly in the ditch, one on top of the other. Luckily, the go-cart spun off in another direction crashing up against the wall of the ditch. We were dazed, but alive!

For a few moments we lay motionless, wondering if there was anything broken. We began to pick ourselves up and realised we had escaped with only cuts and bruises. As we dragged our monster back up the hill and homewards, we were silent. It was to be both its test drive and final outing.

When we parked the monster in the yard, Mother asked us if we had enjoyed ourselves. We looked at each other and nodded unconvincingly. Peter's eyes betrayed a deep sense of shock at his near-death experience. I, too, no longer felt invincible. We both knew we were fortunate that day; we had lived to tell the tale. Our monster was now slowly dismantled and its parts used for other less dangerous exploits. The rest of the summer passed uneventfully; but we were content with that; one life-threatening event was enough!'

Exercise 1: 13

Think of an interesting event you or someone you know has experienced and write about it here.

_____

_____

_____

_____

_____

_____

_____

_____

_____

_____

_____

_____

_____

_____

_____

10. Literature and other Sources

Ideas for writing can come from many different **Sources**.

Inspiration can come from images and words from the arts and visual media such as film, television, photographs, paintings, dance, sculpture, theatre and museums.

Other literary forms such as poetry, plays, novels, historical material, short stories and articles can also provide ideas.

Literature is always a good source. Studying successful writers can inspire great ideas for character and storyline.

© 2008 Stephen Curran

Example:

> Demonstrate how ideas can come from a great novel like **Oliver Twist** by Charles Dickens.

In this extract we join Oliver Twist with the other boys in the workhouse refectory awaiting their daily gruel.

'Oliver Twist and his companions suffered the tortures of slow starvation for three months: at last ... a council was held; lots were cast who should walk up to the master after supper that evening, and ask for more; and it fell to Oliver Twist.

The evening arrived; the boys took their places. The master, in the cook's uniform, stationed himself at the copper; his pauper assistants ranged themselves behind him; the gruel was served out; and a long grace was said over the short commons. The gruel disappeared; the boys whispered each other, and winked at Oliver; while his next neighbours nudged him. Child as he was, he was desperate with hunger, and reckless with misery. He rose from the table; and advancing to the master, basin and spoon in hand, said: somewhat alarmed at his own temerity:

"Please, sir, I want some more."

The master was a fat, healthy man; but he turned very pale. He gazed in stupefied astonishment on the small rebel for some seconds, and then clung for support to the copper. The assistants were paralysed with wonder; the boys with fear.

"What!" said the master at length in a faint voice.

"Please, sir," replied Oliver, "I want some more."

The master aimed a blow at Oliver's head with the ladle; pinioned him in his arms; and shrieked aloud for the beadle.'

Ideas about Characters and Storyline

Details about Oliver could give you ideas for a character: This is a story about an **orphan child**. He is thought to have no living relatives, so he has been sent to a workhouse where he is treated cruelly and sadistically. He is being slowly starved along with the other boys and no one cares. Oliver shows a great deal of bravery when he asks for more gruel.

The **master** is fat and self-satisfied with a violent temper.

The **storyline** will deal with how Oliver escapes a life of poverty, cruelty and potential criminality to be eventually reunited with his wealthy relatives he does not know exist.

A story could be written about a child with no parents who is sent to an orphanage. The child might be treated cruelly by the housemaster in the orphanage and he stands up to him.

Exercise 1: 14

Think of a story you have read or a film you have seen. Make notes about the main characters and the storyline that could inspire your story.

_____

_____

_____

_____

_____

_____

_____

_____

© 2008 Stephen Curran

Your Own Story - Draft One

This is your chance to write your own story using one of the following scenarios as a starting point.

On the next page are two story scenarios.

Choose either:

Story 1 - *The Room*   or   Story 2 - *Trapped*

• Use the learning points in this chapter to help you write.

• Observe the basic rules below to help structure your story.

• Write Story 1 or 2 in this book. Once you have learnt the principles, you can write the other story on separate sheets of paper.

Story Starting Points

Try and include ideas and techniques from this chapter.

1. The Five Senses - sight, hearing, touch, smell and taste

2. Images, Sounds, Objects, Smells & Tastes - experiences

3. The Sixth Sense - feelings

4. Brainstorming Ideas - using lists and spider diagrams

5. 'Stream of Consciousness' - writing without editing

6. Writing in Role - in present tense as the character

7. Special Memories - locations or events

8. Characters from People you Know - people you have met

9. Dramatic Life Events - your life experiences

10. Literature and other Sources - things you have read

Observe these Rules and complete the Story

1. The character is not allowed to leave the space. Find a way to end the story in the space without leaving it.

2. One other character can enter the space and leave it at some point in the story.

3. Write out the scenario first and then continue the story.

22   © 2008 Stephen Curran

First Draft - Story 1

The Room

Opening Scenario in Past Tense:

'I roused from an uneasy sleep. I opened my eyes but it was hard to see anything. There was very little light in the room. Where was I? My heart began to pound. This was not my room. My eyes adjusted to the light. I could just make out the walls of the room. They seemed drab and discoloured. Was I dreaming? It must be a dream. I went to sleep in my own bed. I closed my eyes and opened them again. Still the same; it was not a dream!'

First Draft - Story 2

Trapped

Opening Scenario in Past Tense:

'Everything came crashing down. As I awoke, I knew I was trapped. It was a terrifying moment. The dust settled; I could just make out through the haze a small shaft of light coming from above. I scrambled upwards, but soon found myself sliding back down again. I felt hot and bothered and fumbled around for the bottle of water I had with me. I guzzled it voraciously. Luckily my torch was undamaged. I flicked the switch and the beam pierced the darkness. I started to explore the space. There must be a way out. I yelled; it echoed, but there was no answer.'

Choose to write either **Story 1** or **Story 2**, then use the Planning page to write down some ideas for your story.

© 2008 Stephen Curran

Planning - 1st Draft
Story 1 - *The Room*

Now let's write a story.

If you have chosen **Story 1 - *The Room***, copy out the opening scenario on Story Page 1 - 1st Draft, then continue your story on the pages that follow.

Planning - 1st Draft
Story 2 - *Trapped*

It's time for your own story.

_____

_____

_____

_____

_____

_____

_____

_____

_____

_____

_____

_____

_____

_____

_____

_____

_____

_____

_____

_____

If you have chosen **Story 2 - *Trapped***, copy out the opening scenario on Story Page 1 - 1st Draft, then continue your story on the pages that follow.

© 2008 Stephen Curran

Story Page 1 - 1st Draft
The Room or *Trapped*

Story Page 2 - 1st Draft
The Room or *Trapped*

Intrigue

© 2008 Stephen Curran

Story Page 3 - 1st Draft
The Room or *Trapped*

Story Page 4 - 1st Draft
The Room or *Trapped*

Fright

Story Page 4 - 1st Draft
The Room or *Trapped*

Story Page 5 - 1st Draft
The Room or *Trapped*

Story Page 6 - 1st Draft
The Room or *Trapped*

Terror

Scores Out of Ten	Spelling & Grammar → ☐	Creativity → ☐

© 2008 Stephen Curran

Chapter Two
Literary Devices
1. Developing Description

We can develop our **Descriptions** by focusing on five things:
Sights • Sounds • Scents & Tastes • Textures • Responses

Example:  Using the story title ***The Dark Forest***, write five descriptive phrases for sights, sounds, scents & tastes, textures and responses.

The five forms of description might go something like this:

Sights: *shapes moving in the dark; branches like hands reaching out; dancing shadows; pin-points of lights like eyes; twisted gnarled forms*

Sounds: *crunching leaves; twigs snapping; shuffling; wild animals howling; wind whistling in the trees*

Scents & Tastes: *rotting leaves; pungent flesh from a dead fox; crisp night breeze; cherry blossom; musty air*

Textures: *rough bark; sharp scratching; crumbly moss; thorns; ghostly cobwebs brushing against the face; red itching legs from stinging nettles*

Feeling Responses: *gnawing fear; rising terror; pensive with expectation; looking jumpy; knotted stomach*

Exercise 2: 1   Using ***The Dark Forest***, write four more words or phrases for each of the five sensory categories.

Sights: 1. _____ 2. _____

3. _____ 4. _____

32   © 2008 Stephen Curran

Sounds: 1. _____ 2. _____

3. _____ 4. _____

Scents & Tastes: 1. _____ 2. _____

3. _____ 4. _____

Textures: 1. _____ 2. _____

3. _____ 4. _____

Feeling Responses: 1. _____ 2. _____

3. _____ 4. _____

Think about **The Room** or **Trapped**. In a Second Draft we should try and improve the level of description in the story.

Exercise 2: 2 Thinking about **The Room** or **Trapped**, write four more words or phrases for each of the five sensory categories.

Sights: e.g. *spiders dangling; chiselled graffiti*

1. _____ 2. _____

3. _____ 4. _____

Sounds: e.g. *distant footsteps; muted traffic sounds*

1. _____ 2. _____

3. _____ 4. _____

Scents & Tastes: e.g. *stale urine; rotting sandwich*

1. _____ 2. _____

3. _____ 4. _____

Textures: e.g. *damp walls; rusty bed frame*

1. _____ 2. _____

© 2008 Stephen Curran

3. _____ 4. _____

Feeling Responses: e.g. *increasing anxiety; feeling homesick*

1. _____ 2. _____

3. _____ 4. _____

2. The Flashback

A **Flashback** is an excellent way of finding out more about a character or what has occurred before the story begins. In story terms this is called the **Backstory**. It can refer to what happened just before the story began, or an event further back in the past that has significance for the story that is to be told.

Example: | Using the title ***My Dog Jack***, write a story with a flashback that creates backstory.

'Jack growled at me, baring his teeth yet again. You couldn't even get near him. I thought golden retrievers were supposed to be friendly. This one wasn't! Torn and busted furniture lay strewn around our lounge and it was all Jack's fault. My stepmum stared at me angrily with that 'It's your dog' look. She would do anything she could to get rid of Jack. So much had changed in two short years...

I look down at the cutest and cuddliest puppy ever. He yaps delightedly as I pick him up.

 Dad says, "Tim, it'll make up for Mum leaving."

 The man from the rescue centre nods, "He's yours. You know, he deserves a good home after what he's been through; being found on a dump and all that."

I name him Jack as 'Yap' sounds like Jack. He licks my face lovingly and then starts to bite uncontrollably...

34   © 2008 Stephen Curran

Jack's eyes stared at me menacingly as he chewed my shoe. I remembered what the man had said. What lay behind those cold eyes? What had happened on that dump to make him so vicious and aggressive?

My stepmum pointed at Jack, "Get rid of it or else!"'

Note: The main story has been told in the past tense and the flashback in the present tense. This is an effective literary device because it reverses what the audience or reader expects (i.e. they would expect you to tell the present in present tense and the past in past tense).

Now think of **The Room** or **Trapped**. A flashback could focus on:

• Where the main character was before he or she found themselves alone in this room or space.

• A past memory that reveals some important detail about the main character and their life beforehand.

The **Transition to a Flashback** is usually shown with ... (an ellipsis) and then a new paragraph. Ways into a flashback could be *'He daydreamed...'* or *'She cast her mind back...'* or *'The room began to spin...'* etc.

Exercise 2: 3 Think about **The Room** or **Trapped** and write an effective flashback.

Write your flashback here: _____

_____

_____

_____

_____

_____

© 2008 Stephen Curran

_____

_____

_____

_____

3. The Flashforward

A **Flashforward** is an opportunity for the story to take an imaginary or a real time leap into the future.

An **Imaginary Flashforward** means the character will either imagine in a moment of reflection or have a dream about a possible future event that is significant to the story.

A **Real Time Flashforward** means time will pass and the story will move to a future event and continue to be told from that point onwards.

Example:  | Write an imaginary flashforward for *My Dog Jack*.

In *My Dog Jack*, we could have our character Tina taking Jack to the vet to be put down and then she could **imagine a future scene** by the graveside.

'*My stepmum's lip curled with sardonic pleasure as she dumped Jack's carrying box on the table. He yelped and growled as he was coaxed out. Dad wouldn't even discuss it at home. He's really weak and she tells him what to do.*

All he said was, "Tim, you're ten, she knows best."

I stood beside the vet as he raised the needle. He said he had to do it if my stepmum said he had attacked people. He asked if I wanted to say goodbye to Jack for the last time.

Those words left me cold and I felt dizzy and sick...

Tears run down my face as I stand by a shallow pile of earth heaped up near a windswept tree.

> *I whisper, "I didn't mean it Jack, sorry. She made me!"*
I turn away from the grave and I feel woozy...

A nurse steadied me. The syringe with its lethal dose was still hovering over Jack's sedated form.

> *"No!" I yelled, "You mustn't do it! She's lying, Jack never hurt anybody."'*

Note: It is again very effective to use the past tense for the present and the present tense for the future.

A **Real Time Flashforward** shows that time has passed and the story is taken up again at a future point.

Example: | Write a real time flashforward for ***My Dog Jack***.

'A nurse steadied me. The syringe with its lethal dose was still hovering over Jack's sedated form.

> *"No!" I yelled, "You mustn't do it! She's lying, Jack never hurt anybody."*
Then it was all over. Jack lay there motionless...

A year passes:
I stand by a shallow pile of earth heaped up near a windswept tree. Tears run down my face.

> *I mouth, "I didn't mean it Jack, sorry! She made me!"*
I place Jack's favourite toy by the grave. All I can see is Jack's sad eyes in those last moments. I slowly walk away from the grave. I notice my stepmum approaching. She is all smiles. I hate her now more than ever...'

© 2008 Stephen Curran

Now think of a flashforward for **The Room** or **Trapped**. Either an imaginary or real time flashforward could be written. An **Imaginary Flashforward** might involve the character dreaming or thinking about his or her own family sitting round the table on his or her birthday and remembering him or her. A **Real Time Flashforward** might involve the character still being in the room or space for years to come. He or she would now be old and grey and perhaps there would be dozens of carved notches on the wall showing many years had passed.

The **transition to an imaginary flashforward** is shown in a similar way to a flashback with ... (an ellipsis).

The **transition to a real time flashforward** is usually introduced with a time statement like *'Many years pass'* or with a title like *20 Years Later* or *May 2027*.

Exercise 2: 4

Try writing an effective flashforward for **The Room** or **Trapped**.

Write your flashforward here: _____

_____

_____

_____

_____

_____

_____

_____

_____

_____

4. Tension

Tension in a story can be compared to a 'slow burn candle'. Events must keep occurring in the story to hold the interest of the reader. These can be understood as either **complications** in the plot (storyline) or **problems** the main character has to face and solve.

Throughout the story the pressure must be kept up and maintained otherwise interest will be lost. However, the tension can vary in its level of intensity. It is like watching a tennis match. It is a more exciting match to spectate if the players are continually putting each other under pressure.

Example:  Write a story called **The Tunnel**. Maintain the tension by building in problems that put the main character under pressure.

'Sweat poured down my face. The air was so thin. I could just make out there was a bend in the tunnel up ahead. Just as I reached the bend, my torch suddenly dimmed. I knew the battery was nearly out. Then, to my horror, I found myself in a low, cavern-like space. There were five different tunnels leading off it. Which one should I take? I had no idea. Now I knew I was really lost. The torch flickered and it suddenly went black.'

It is important to make things happen in **The Room** or **Trapped** to maintain the level of tension. Remember one character could enter the room or space, a meal could be delivered, things could be found in the room or space (maybe some bones), an escape attempt could be foiled or an action-filled flashback or flashforward could be built in.

© 2008 Stephen Curran

Exercise 2: 5 Write about your character in **The Room** or **Trapped** and maintain the tension by making things happen.

5. Suspense

Suspense can be compared to a 'quick burn firework'. Suspense occurs when tension is built quickly and there is much more at stake for the characters.

It often involves a life-threatening situation for the main character. Tension created through suspense is usually released quickly. Suspense is only effective if it is used more sparingly in stories.

Example:  | Using ***The Tunnel***, create suspense by building events to a tense climax.

In ***The Tunnel***, we can build the suspense gradually by creating a series of events that put the main character under more and more pressure until we reach a climax where something terrible might happen. We rejoin the character as he attempts to escape from some assailants.

'As I ran faster, I could see there was a bend in the tunnel up ahead. I could hear footsteps coming from somewhere in the tunnel system. They were getting louder and I could now discern voices. They would kill me if they found me. I gasped heavily and sweat poured down my face. The air was so thin. Just as I reached the bend, my torch suddenly dimmed. I knew the battery was nearly out.

Then, to my horror, I found myself in a low, cavern-like space. There were five different tunnels leading off it. The sound of men approaching was now deafening, but coming from which tunnel? I had no idea. The torch flickered and it suddenly went black. Terror gripped me as the sound of footsteps drew closer. The thud of my beating heart crashed into my ears. Which tunnel? Was I in the wrong part of the cavern? I felt completely helpless. I wanted to scream!'

In ***The Room*** or ***Trapped***, suspense can be built in a number of different ways. Perhaps the character who enters the room or space could threaten or endanger the main character and this causes uncertainty and fear. Maybe the room or space begins to fill up with water or choking fumes and the character cannot escape. The main character could also risk their life even more to escape from the room or space.

© 2008 Stephen Curran

Exercise 2: 6 Write about your character in **The Room** or **Trapped**. Build the suspense by bringing the situation to a climax.

6. Anticipation

Anticipation is when there is a strong inkling of what might happen next. A high level of tension or suspense does not neccesarily mean a reader will know exactly what is coming next, but it is often something life-threatening. For example, if someone is swimming in the sea and sharks are encircling them, only the dorsal fins might be seen. However, that is enough for a reader to anticipate a scene of carnage and imagine the fear of being eaten.

42   © 2008 Stephen Curran

Example:  | Using *My Dog Jack*, create a sense of anticipation about Jack's impending death.

Anticipation in a scene gives us a sense of what will happen next. We know that Jack might die in this scene and this fear of what might happen drives the scene. Anticipation of an event raises the level of tension significantly.

'A nurse steadied me. **The syringe with its lethal dose was still hovering over Jack's sedated form.**

   "No!" I yelled, "You mustn't do it! She's lying, Jack never hurt anybody."

The vet hesitated and cast a glance in my direction.

   "Don't listen to her; that dog's a menace. You ought to have seen the torn and scarred flesh of the child it attacked. It was horrible. That poor child."

She pulled a face and made to cry.

   The vet turned back to me, "Any last goodbyes? It's time, I've got things to do."

I was too shocked to respond. I peered round at the determined faces in the room for some glint of mercy or hope. Jack's breath was shallow and his tongue lolled from the corner of his mouth. Surely they would listen to reason and give Jack just one more chance. Why were they doing this?

I made to rush forward and stop the vet, but found my arms securely clenched. I struggled but it was useless. The nurse that stopped me from fainting tightened her grip.

The syringe began to descend slowly toward Jack's leg. My stepmum's eyes brightened and she looked right at me. They were dry. She would shed no tears over Jack. I knew I was beaten; I could do nothing. Closer and closer; the needle touched Jacks fur. It plunged in; he twitched and lay still. It was over!'

© 2008 Stephen Curran

Exercise 2: 7 Think of an event that could happen in **The Room** or **Trapped**. Build the anticipation that leads to this event.

_____

_____

_____

_____

_____

_____

_____

_____

_____

_____

_____

_____

_____

_____

_____

7. Mood

Mood refers to the particular state of mind of one of the central characters. The way that character feels will then dominate the whole storyline. If the main character is sad then this mood is communicated to the reader or audience.

Example:
 Write a story called **Lost**, which demonstrates the main character's mood is one of panic.

44 © 2008 Stephen Curran

'The train doors slid closed. Just a moment before, Paul had been holding his mother's hand. Now she was on the other side of the glass. Terror filled his mind; he had lost his mummy and he might never see her again.

He had dashed excitedly through the open doors thinking she would follow, but it was the wrong train. She had seemed too busy looking for the right one and had let his hand slip from hers. The carriage began to move slowly away from the platform and then it sped up. It was soon in the tunnel. Paul pushed his way through to the doors and bashed his hands against them. No one seemed to notice his tiny form, as the train was so crowded. Their noses were in their newspapers and they avoided each other's gaze. Paul tried to prise open the doors but the train then lurched to the right and he was squashed between people's legs and against the doors. **Paul felt a choking feeling rising up in his throat.**

He began to cry for his mummy, but the pounding and deafening noise of the train obscured his wails. He pushed and tugged at everything and everyone around him, but there was no response. He screamed and screamed, but the train screeched louder as it moved over the points. His lungs were no match. Paul felt he was drowning in noise and heat. His breathing became short and shallow as panic coursed through his veins.'

Now think of **The Room** or **Trapped**. There is an opportunity for the character to show any number of moods that might dominate the storyline. The character might panic initially when he realises he cannot escape from the room. This might give way to a mood of depression when he feels

© 2008 Stephen Curran

like giving up. The main character might exude fear if the other character who enters the room acts in a threatening or suspicious manner. Fear might grow into terror if a direct threat is made.

Exercise 2: 8

Think about **The Room** or *Trapped*. Give your main character a mood that will pervade part of the story.

_____

_____

_____

_____

_____

_____

_____

_____

_____

_____

_____

_____

8. Atmosphere

Atmosphere in scientific terms refers to the gaseous environment (oxygen, carbon dioxide, etc.) that makes life possible on earth. In a story, atmosphere refers to the general tone or feeling that has been created by the writer, but it does not necessarily come specifically from the characters.

Example:  Create a dreamy, nostalgic and sentimental atmosphere in the story ***The Christmas Lights***.

This story is about a young girl who has a mysterious encounter with Father Christmas on Christmas Eve.

'*Angie stood on the corner of the busy street holding her father's hand.* **O Little Town of Bethlehem** *blared from a nearby speaker. Shoppers with bright, expectant faces, laden with last minute shopping of every kind, dashed by. Angie stared up above her. The dazzling rainbow haze of lights glowed through the falling snow.*

Angie felt lonely because she had no brothers or sisters to play with, and being in a new school meant she had no friends either. As she looked again at the bright dancing forms they seemed to offer hope. In particular, the massive display of a jubilant Father Christmas, with dancing elves and galloping reindeer, began to make her feel warm inside. She looked across the street and noticed two children playing in the snow. They were having such fun dodging snowballs and sliding on the icy patches. The sound of their laughter mingled with a sudden gust of wind. Angie again felt the chill and it seemed to reach right within her.

The red and white lights of the dancing Father Christmas cast delicate shadows across the drifting snow. *Her father pointed to some of the other lights but Angie was completely transfixed. In the heavy air everything seemed to blur. All Angie could see was the face of the Father Christmas and it was as if her eyes had telephoto lenses. She could now make out his lips were moving and she could hear, above all the bustle of the street, the soft but penetrating words:*

© 2008 Stephen Curran

"Make a wish and it will come true."
Now she was focusing on his eyes and they were kind and inviting.
*Angie made the wish **and she suddenly felt as if her whole body**
was being bathed in light and warmth.'*

Think about ***The Room*** or ***Trapped***. If we create an atmosphere with echoing footsteps, bars on the windows, an iron bedstead and a peephole in the door, it would feel like we were in a cell instead of a room. An enclosed, suffocating atmosphere could be created by a low ceiling. Falling masonry could indicate someone was trapped in a collapsed building.

Exercise 2: 9

Create atmosphere in a section of ***The Room*** or ***Trapped*** through the events of the story.

___

© 2008 Stephen Curran

9. Conflict

For a story to work there must be **Conflict** right from the start. **Conflict between the characters is essential.** Always make the characters want different things and then they will have disagreements. Even characters who are on the same side should have different perspectives and views. There can also be conflict with nature, e.g. climbing a very dangerous mountain; a serious fire; the dangers of the sea; etc.

Example: Write a story called ***The Sad Clown*** which shows characters in conflicting situations.

In the story ***The Sad Clown***, a little orphan boy visits the circus repeatedly in one week to see his favourite clown. After the performance he tries to find Coco.

'Billy approaches the Big Top with trepidation. Where is Coco the clown? His flowing white costume, painted face and big red nose always made him feel happy. During the performance the day before, he had laughed until tears of joy streamed down his cheeks, but where was Coco today?

It was the last day of the circus. Soon they would take him back to the orphanage; back to that lonely, cold room. He had to find Coco first.

He sees Coco alone by the side of the Big Top with his head in his hands. Billy feels scared, but he reaches out a friendly hand. Coco draws back.

"I'm not funny anymore," Coco blurts.

Billy considers, "I still laugh at you."

Coco continues, without hearing Billy, "No one laughs at my pranks. They just giggle because I'm too old and pathetic to be a clown anymore."

Billy protests, "But I love the prat falls; the jokes that don't work properly."

© 2008 Stephen Curran

49

"That's just it, they don't work and you're just one little kid. What do you know?"

Billy pulls away. Coco looks up suddenly and sees Billy's eyes fill with tears.

"Sorry, I didn't mean that."

Billy turns and runs away, crying uncontrollably.'

In **The Room** or **Trapped** conflict needs to be created between the main character and the character that enters the room or space. Conflict can also occur through encounters with characters in flashback or flashforward situations.

Exercise 2: 10

Think about **The Room** or **Trapped**. Rewrite the meeting between your main character and the other character.

_____

_____

_____

_____

_____

_____

_____

_____

_____

_____

_____

_____

_____

10. Surprise

Surprise is a useful story device. This is when something totally unexpected happens in a story.

It can involve the main character finding or discovering something. Perhaps the character is subjected to some capture or assault without warning. They could be presented with a gift that is unusual or find themselves in a strange or weird situation.

Example:  Using **Lost**, create a big surprise by building a totally unexpected event into the story.

This story is about a young boy who seems to be separated accidentally from his mother at an underground station. A surprise awaits the reader as they find out this is not true.

'*No one seemed to notice his tiny form, as the train was so crowded. Their noses were in their newspapers and they avoided each other's gaze. Paul tried to prise open the doors but the train then lurched to the right and he was squashed between people's legs and against the doors. Paul felt a choking feeling rising up in his throat.*

He began to cry for his mummy, but the pounding and deafening noise of the train obscured his wails. He pushed and tugged at everything and everyone around him, but there was no response. He screamed and screamed, but the train screeched louder as it moved over the points. His lungs were no match. Paul felt he was drowning in noise and heat. His breathing became short and shallow as panic coursed through his veins.

*On the platform there was a scene of calm. **Patricia walked slowly away from the platform edge and up the stairs. There was no*** *panicking mother or lost child calls. Paul had not realised, but his mother had deliberately let go of his hand.*

As she casually walked away, her lip curled in a wry smile. She had never wanted Paul; the nappies, the tummy aches, the vomiting, the endless 'Mummy this' and 'Mummy that' had annoyed her intensely. Quite frankly, he was a nuisance and he stopped her enjoying herself. It was that stupid husband, Tom, who had wanted the baby. She never did.'

Exercise 2: 11

Think of a surprising or unexpected event that could happen in **The Room** or **Trapped** and write it here.

11. Intrigue or Curiosity

Intrigue or **Curiosity** is created in a story when something mysterious or strange happens. Human beings are naturally curious and inquisitive and will want to solve a mystery.

For example, interest and fascination is created immediately by using magical and incredible elements in a story.

Example: Using *The Christmas Lights*, create a sense of intrigue and curiosity in the reader.

We return to the story just before Angie has a mysterious encounter with Father Christmas on Christmas Eve.

'The red and white lights of the dancing Father Christmas cast delicate shadows across the drifting snow. Her father pointed to some of the other lights but Angie was completely transfixed. In the heavy air everything seemed to blur. All Angie could see was the face of the Father Christmas and it was as if her eyes had telephoto lenses. She could now make out his lips were moving and she could hear, above all the bustle of the street, the soft but penetrating words:

> **"Make a wish and it will come true."**

Now she was focusing on his eyes and they were kind and inviting. Angie made the wish and she suddenly felt as if her whole body was being bathed in light and warmth. Angie tugged at her father's hand; he looked up and smiled at the spectacle, but to him it was just a haze of bright lights.

Angie went to her bed eagerly that night. Her mother was surprised she did not want to stay up as she usually did. Straight after her cocoa she rushed to her bedroom excited. **She snuggled down into the bedclothes, awaiting the fulfilment of the promise. Angie soon drifted into the world of her dreams. Then, and only then, did the epic journey begin... Angie felt herself rising.**

© 2008 Stephen Curran

She sat up and realised she was high above the clouds; she was floating on a bed of snow. She scooped up the white powder in her hands; it did not feel cold at all. Angie could see the lights of the city far below. As she looked up again she saw she was approaching a huge, iron gate. It slowly opened as she drew near. Beyond the gate lay a beautiful hilly landscape covered in a blanket of crisp white snow. The night was drawing in and the fading light seemed to turn blue as it reflected on the icy scene.

Angie circled the landscape on the blanket of snow and then she found herself gradually descending. A tall and rotund figure stood by a large conifer tree laden with thick snow and surrounded with mist. He looked familiar, but Angie knew she had never met him before. In a moment she found herself standing before him. He beckoned her to accompany him. As he stepped aside she saw a gleaming, golden sleigh.

He climbed onto the sleigh; Angie hesitated, then joined him. The mist cleared to reveal a team of reindeer. They bristled and stamped their hoofs in the cold air. When she looked again at the man he was pulling on his big red overcoat. He glanced at her and his wrinkled face spread into a full smile. His deep blue eyes glinted with kindness in the waning light.

"We have a long journey to make before nightfall."
He flicked the reins and the sleigh was soon speeding through the sparse landscape.

It began to snow heavily and a biting wind cut into their faces. Through the white haze massive oak doors appeared. They opened wide as the party sped through. They screeched to a halt. Angie followed the bearded man, ascended a wide, curved stairway and

54   © 2008 Stephen Curran

entered a huge hall bathed with light. Tall classical pillars like those in Greek temples lined the edges of the hall.

Suddenly an excited cheer rang out and they were surrounded by what seemed like small children.

A chant echoed though the hall, "Santa! Santa!"
The tall, bearded old man turned to Angie.

"Welcome to the Kingdom of the Elves."
One tiny elf in a pointed hat was urged forward by the others. He bowed before Angie and slowly offered a posy of flowers. For a moment he stood motionless; his eyes were downcast.

"Come on Timmy, don't be shy," Santa urged.

"To, to our snow... princess," he stammered.

Angie protested, "But I'm just an ordinary girl!"

"Well, no one is just ordinary here. We're all special here, aren't we Timmy?" Santa placed a reassuring hand on his shoulder. He turned to Angie, "He's the shyest of all, in my army of elves. Now, Timmy, you'll show our guest all the treasures of the kingdom and we'll prepare the banquet."

Santa moved off and joined the throng of elves. In a flash he disappeared behind another huge set of doors. Angie looked down at Timmy and he turned away bashfully.

"Well, Timmy, I suppose I'd better have a tour."
Timmy moved off slowly to the side of the hall. A partition opened and a huge treasure store appeared. Lit by candles, hundreds of gold and silver objects gleamed; rubies and diamonds shone like stars; a magnificent golden crown stood on a plinth.

"You have so much wealth!" Angie commented.

"It buys all the materials to make presents."
Timmy took Angie up a winding staircase onto a platform and

© 2008 Stephen Curran

another partition drew back. *A whole factory of elves were furiously working; the sound of hammers, drills and lathes was deafening.*

"It's nearly Christmas. They may not be ready in time."

Angie surveyed the amazing scene, "Don't you help?"

"No!" Timmy whispered, "They say I break the toys."
Suddenly everything stopped. The elves rolled out a long red carpet and Santa strolled into the middle and beckoned Angie and Timmy join him.

"It's time," Santa announced. "Fetch the crown."'

Exercise 2: 12

Think of an intriguing or mysterious event that could happen in **The Room** or **Trapped** and write it here.

Your Own Story - Draft Two

This is your chance to continue your own story using your chosen scenario as a starting point.

Continue either:

Story 1 - *The Room* or **Story 2 - *Trapped***

• Use the learning points in this chapter to help you write.

• Observe the basic rules below to help structure your story.

• Write Story 1 or 2 in this book. Once you have learnt the principles, you can write the other story on separate sheets of paper.

Literary Devices

Include ideas and techniques from the topics so far.

1. Developing Description - using the senses
2. The Flashback - a past memory providing backstory
3. The Flashforward - imaginary or real time event
4. Tension - slow burn
5. Suspense - quick burn
6. Anticipation - we know a particular thing will happen
7. Mood - state of mind of one of the characters
8. Atmosphere - general tone or feeling
9. Conflict - permeates the story at every level
10. Surprise - something unexpected happens
11. Intrigue or Curiosity - something mysterious happens

Observe these Rules and complete the Story

1. The character is not allowed to leave the space. Find a way to end the story in the space without leaving it.
2. One other character can enter the space and leave it at some point in the story.
3. Write out the scenario first and then continue the story.

© 2008 Stephen Curran

Second Draft - Story 1

The Room

Opening Scenario in Present Tense:

'I rouse from an uneasy sleep. I open my eyes, but it is hard to see anything. There is very little light in the room. Where am I? My heart begins to pound. This is not my room. My eyes adjust to the light. I can just make out the walls of the room. They seem drab and discoloured. Am I dreaming? It must be a dream. I went to sleep in my own bed. I close my eyes and open them again. Still the same; it is not a dream!'

Second Draft - Story 2

Trapped

Opening Scenario in Present Tense:

'Everything comes crashing down. As I awake, I know I am trapped. It is a terrifying moment. The dust settles; I can just make out through the haze a small shaft of light coming from above. I scramble upwards, but soon find myself sliding back down again. I feel hot and bothered and fumble around for the bottle of water I have with me. I guzzle it voraciously. Luckily my torch is undamaged. I flick the switch and the beam pierces the darkness. I start to explore the space. There must be a way out. I yell; it echoes, but there is no answer.'

Continue with either **Story 1** or **Story 2**, then use the Planning page to write down some more ideas for your story.

Planning - 2nd Draft
Story 1 - *The Room*

Let's plan a second draft.

If you chose **Story 1 - *The Room***, copy out the opening scenario on Story Page 1 - 2nd Draft, then continue your story on the pages that follow.

Planning - 2nd Draft
Story 2 - *Trapped*

It's time to plan a second draft.

If you chose **Story 2 - *Trapped***, copy out the opening scenario on Story Page 1 - 2nd Draft, then continue your story on the pages that follow.

Story Page 1 - 2nd Draft
The Room or *Trapped*

Shock

© 2008 Stephen Curran

Story Page 2 - 2nd Draft
The Room or *Trapped*

Story Page 3 - 2nd Draft
The Room or *Trapped*

Concern

© 2008 Stephen Curran

Story Page 4 - 2nd Draft
The Room or *Trapped*

Fright

Story Page 5 - 2nd Draft
The Room or *Trapped*

Panic

Story Page 6 - 2nd Draft
The Room or *Trapped*

Terror

Scores Out of Ten	Spelling & Grammar → ☐	Creativity → ☐

Marking the Stories

If you are working with a teacher, tutor or an experienced adult the stories can be given a Creativity and a Spelling & Grammar mark.

Mark Scheme (marks 1 to 10)

Outstanding	**10 marks**	*Acceptable*	**5 marks**
Excellent	**9 marks**	*Needs some work*	**4 marks**
Very Good	**8 marks**	*Needs a lot of work*	**3 marks**
Good	**7 marks**	*Requires more effort*	**2 marks**
Satisfactory	**6 marks**	*Rework it completely*	**1 mark**

A mark below **5** means the story should be attempted again.

	Spelling & Grammar	**Creativity**
*Story 1 - **The Room*** *First Draft*	☐	☐
*Story 2 - **Trapped*** *First Draft*	☐	☐
*Story 1 - **The Room*** *Second Draft*	☐	☐
*Story 2 - **Trapped*** *Second Draft*	☐	☐

Total Score ☐ **+** Total Score ☐

Average Score out of 10 (Divide total by 8) ☐

Overall Percentage ☐ **%**

Total Score ☐

ⓐⓔ © 2008 Stephen Curran

CERTIFICATE OF

ACHIEVEMENT

This certifies

_____

has successfully completed

KS2 Creative Writing
Year 6
WORKBOOK 1

Overall percentage
score achieved

%

Comment _____

_____

Signed _____

(teacher/parent/guardian)

Date _____